Studying God's Word:
An Everyday Guide to the Bible

By
Apostle Charles A. Daniels

PRESS

Studying God's Word: An Everyday Guide to the Bible
by Apostle Charles A. Daniels

Printed in the United States of America

ISBN 9781622300679

Unless otherwise indicated, Bible quotations are taken from The Layman's Parallel New Testament Comparing four popular translations in parallel columns. Copyright © 1970 by Zondervan Publishing House, Grand Rapids, Michigan.

www.xulonpress.com

Acknowledgements

I offer my deepest thanks and gratitude to:

New Beginnings International Ministries -- thank you for your prayers and financial support. Thanks for being a ministry that has a desire for the Kingdom of God.

My wife, Elaine for enduring the time it took me to write this book. Thank you for making my life complete.

His Servant, Apostle Charles A. Daniels

TABLE OF CONTENTS

TAB E

New Beginnings International Ministries

Bible Training Conference Learning Objectives

- Learn how to apply the Word of God to your life

- Learn to value the integrity of God's Word

- Learn how to study the Bible

- Learn how to live by the Word of God

- Learn the benefits of reading, hearing, studying, memorizing and meditating upon the Word of God

- Learn how to abide in the Word of God

- Learn how to meditate upon the Word of God

- Learn how to use a Bible concordance

- Learn how to use a Bible dictionary

- Learn the purpose of a Bible atlas

- Learn the purpose of a Bible commentary

- Learn how to pray the Scriptures

Group Activities for Conference Attendees

- What does the word *integrity* mean, according to Webster's dictionary?

- What does Jesus say a man should live by other than bread, according to Matthew 4:4?

- According 1 Peter 1:22-25, how is a person "born again"? Please write out the Scripture verses.

- According to John 3:3-5, how can a man enter into or see the kingdom of God?

- According to Colossians 1:13-14, what happens when a person is "born again"?

- According to Romans 12:1-2, how can a man be transformed from the world into the kingdom of God?

- According to Isaiah 55:8-11, what does the prophet Isaiah say about God's Word?

- According to John 1:1-3 and Revelation 19:13, who is called the Word of God?

- What does the word *logos* mean in the Greek?

- What does the word *rhema* mean in the Greek?

- How many books are in the Bible?

- Using a Vine's Bible concordance, define the word *hear* as recorded in Mark 4:20.

- Using a Bible concordance and Webster's dictionary, define the word *hear* as recorded in Romans 10:17.

- How can a believer receive faith, according to Romans 10:17?

- According to Revelation 1:3, what promises are recorded, and what are the conditions for receiving the promises?

- Using Strong's Bible concordance, define the Greek word for readeth as recorded in Revelation 1:3. What is the Strong's number listed in Vine's concordance for readeth?

- Define the word *study* as recorded in 2 Timothy 2:15, using a Vine's concordance, Bible dictionary and Webster's dictionary.

- What does the word *memorized* mean, according to Webster's dictionary?

- What does Psalm 119:9-11 say? What are we to do with the Word of God according to Psalm 119:11?

- According Joshua 1:8, what are the three listed keys to success?

- According to Vine's concordance, what is the Hebrew word *meditate* mean recorded in Joshua 1:8 ? What is the Strong's number?

- What does the Word of God say about meditating upon the Word day and night? See Psalm 1:2-3.

- What is the purpose of a Bible atlas?

- Who is the founder of the Amplified Bible?

- When was the Amplified Bible founded?

- What is the purpose of the Amplified Bible translation?

- What type of Bible is the New Living Translation?

- How many times is the word *meditate* or *meditation* recorded in the Bible?

- What is the purpose of a Bible commentary?

- Is the King James Version the only translation of the Bible?

- What does Psalm 33:6, 9 record?

- According to Vine's concordance, what does the term *the breath of His mouth* mean in the original Hebrew?

- What does the Greek word for inspira*tion* recorded in 2 Timothy 3:16, according to Vine's concordance?

New Beginnings International Ministries

Bible Training Conference

"For Ezra had prepared his heart to seek the Law of the Lord, and to do it, and to teach statutes and ordinances in Israel" (Ezra 7:10).

CONFERENCE AGENDA

FRIDAY

6:00 p.m. - 6:30 p.m.	Prayer, Praise and Worship
6:30 p.m. - 7:30 p.m.	The Integrity of God's Word
7:30 p.m. - 7:45 p.m.	**BREAK**
7:45 p.m. - 8:45 p.m.	The Blessing of Reading the Word of God

SATURDAY

9:00 a.m. - 9:30 a.m.	Prayer, Praise and Worship
9:30 a.m. - 10:15 a.m.	The Blessing of Hearing the Word of God
10:15 a.m. - 10:30 a.m.	**BREAK**
10:30 a.m. - 11:15 a.m.	How to Study the Bible, Part I
11:15 a.m. – 11:30 a.m.	**BREAK**
11:30 a.m. -12:15 p.m.	How to Study the Bible, Part II - Tools Needed (to Study the Bible)
12:15 p.m. - 1:30 p.m.	**LUNCH**
1:30 p.m. - 2:15 p.m.	The Blessing of Memorizing the Word of God
2:15 p.m. - 2:30 p.m.	**BREAK**
2:30 p.m. - 3:15 p.m.	How to Meditate upon the Word of God

Books of the Bible

Old Testament – (39 Books)	New Testament – (27 Books)
➢ Genesis	➢ Matthew
➢ Exodus	➢ Mark
➢ Leviticus	➢ Luke
➢ Numbers	➢ John
➢ Deuteronomy	➢ Acts
➢ Joshua	➢ Romans
➢ Judges	➢ 1 Corinthians
➢ Ruth	➢ 2 Corinthians
➢ 1 Samuel	➢ Galatians
➢ 2 Samuel	➢ Ephesians
➢ 1 Kings	➢ Philippians
➢ 2 Kings	➢ Colossians
➢ 1 Chronicles	➢ 1 Thessalonians
➢ 2 Chronicles	➢ 2 Thessalonians
➢ Ezra	➢ 1 Timothy
➢ Nehemiah	➢ 2 Timothy
➢ Esther	➢ Titus
➢ Job	➢ Philemon
➢ Psalms	➢ Hebrews
➢ Proverbs	➢ James
➢ Ecclesiastes	➢ 1 Peter
➢ Song of Solomon	➢ 2 Peter
➢ Isaiah	➢ 1 John
➢ Jeremiah	➢ 2 John
➢ Lamentations	➢ 3 John
➢ Ezekiel	➢ Jude
➢ Daniel	➢ Revelation
➢ Hosea	
➢ Joel	
➢ Amos	
➢ Obadiah	
➢ Jonah	
➢ Micah	
➢ Nahum	
➢ Habakkuk	
➢ Zephaniah	
➢ Haggai	
➢ Zechariah	
➢ Malachi	

WHY STUDY THE BIBLE

Introduction: The Bible is the most sold book in the world. Many believers own one, but many don't take the time to read and study it. Studying the Bible allows believers to feed their spirits and keep themselves clean and gain wisdom, knowledge and direction.

I. **TO FEED YOUR SPIRIT ON THE WORD OF GOD**

   A. **Matthew 4:4 -** New International Version (NIV): "Jesus answered, 'It is written: "Man shall not live on bread alone, but on every word that comes from the mouth of God."'"

   - **It is written.**

   - **Man shall not live on bread** alone.

   - Every word that comes from the mouth of God.

   B. **Matthew 4:4** New Living Translation (NLT) - "But Jesus told him, 'No! The Scriptures say, "People do not live by bread alone, but by every word that comes from the mouth of God."'"

   1. We were saved by the Word; we must live every day by the **Word of God.**

   2. Your born-again spirit is designed to live by the **Word of God.**

   3. The **Word of God** provides nourishment for our spirit man.

   4. The **Word of God** is heavenly bread for our souls.

   5. Jesus is the Word of life.

   6. **1 John 1:1-4** (NIV) – "That which was from the beginning, which we have heard, which we have seen with our eyes, which we have looked at and our hands have touched—this we proclaim concerning the Word of life. The life appeared; we have seen it and testify to it, and we proclaim to you the eternal life, which was with the Father and has appeared to us. We proclaim to you what we have seen and heard, so that you also may have fellowship with us. And our fellowship is with the Father and with his Son, Jesus Christ. We write this to make our joy complete."

   C. **1 Peter 2:2** King James Version (KJV) – "As **newborn** babes, **desire** the **sincere** milk of the word, that ye may **grow** thereby."

- **Newborn** (Greek) *artigennetos* means just born or newborn.

- **Desire** (Greek) *epipotheom* means greatly desire, long, earnestly desire, long after, greatly long after, lust, desire, longed after, to long for, desire to pursue with love and to long after.

- **Sincere** (Greek) *adolos* means guileless, in things: unmixed, unadulterated, pure, in persons: without dishonest intent.

- **Grow** (Greek) *auxanoto* means cause to grow, augment, to increase, become greater, of a multitude of people and of inward Christian growth.

  a. We live our spiritual lives by the Word of God.

  b. The Word of God causes us to grow into the things of God.

D. **1 Peter 2:2** (NLT) – "Like newborn babies, you must **crave pure spiritual milk** so that you will **grow into a full experience of salvation. Cry out for this nourishment.**"

- Crave pure spiritual milk.

- Grow into a full experience of salvation.

- Cry out for this nourishment

  1. We must have a strong desire and craving for the Word of God.

  2. Blessed are they that hunger and thirst after righteousness.

  3. There must be a continual hunger and thirst for the Word of God.

E. **Jeremiah 15:16** (KJV) - "Thy words were found and I did eat them and thy word was unto me the joy and rejoicing of mine heart: for I am called by thy name, O Lord God of hosts."

F. **Deuteronomy 8:3** (KJV) – "And he humbled thee, and suffered thee to hunger, and fed thee with manna, which thou knewest not, neither did thy fathers know; that he might make thee know that man doth not live by bread only, but by every word that proceedeth out of the mouth of the Lord doth man live."

G. **1 Thessalonians 2:13** (KJV) – "For this cause also thank we God without ceasing, because, when ye received the word of God which ye heard of us, ye received it not as the word of men, but as it is in truth, the word of God, which effectually worketh also in you that believe."

H. **Job 23:12** (KJV) – "Neither have I gone back from the commandment of his lips; I have esteemed the words of his mouth more than my necessary food."

II. **TO KEEP YOURSELF CLEAN**

A. **John 15:3** (KJV) – "Now ye are **clean** through the **word** which I have spoken unto you."

1. **Clean** (Greek) *katharosin* means a similitude, like a vine cleansed by pruning and so fitted to bear fruit, free from corrupt desire, from sin and guilt, free from every admixture of what is false, sincere, genuine, blameless, innocent, unstained with the guilt of anything.

2. **Word** (Greek) *laleo* means to use words in order to declare one's mind and disclose one's thoughts.

3. The Word of God can **cleanse** our souls.

4. The Word of God can **cleanse** our ways.

5. The Word of God can **cleanse** us from any sin.

B. **John 15:3** (AMP) – "You are cleansed and pruned already, because of the word which I have given you [the teachings I have discussed with you]."

C. **John 17:17** (AMP) – "**Sanctify** them [**purify**, **consecrate**, **separate** them for yourself, and make them holy] by the truth; your **word is truth**."

- Sanctify

- Purify

- Consecrate

- Separate

- The Word is truth.

D. **Ephesians 5:25-26** (NIV) – "Husbands, love your wives, just as Christ loved the church and gave himself up for her to make her holy, cleansing her by the washing with water through the word."

III. **TO GET THE WISDOM OF GOD**

A. **2 Timothy 3:14-16** (NIV) – "But as for you, continue in what you have learned and have become convinced of, because you know those from whom you learned it, and how from infancy you have known the Holy Scriptures, which are able to make you wise for salvation through faith in Christ Jesus. **All Scripture is God-breathed** and is **useful for teaching, rebuking, correcting** and **training in righteousness**."

- All Scripture is God-breathed.

- Useful for teaching

- Rebuking

- Correcting

- Training in righteousness

B. **Proverbs 4:7** (AMP) – "The beginning of Wisdom is: get Wisdom (skillful and godly Wisdom)! [For skillful and godly **Wisdom** is the principal thing.] And with all you have gotten, get understanding (discernment, comprehension and interpretation)."

1. **Wisdom** *is* guided knowledge that can be applied to your life.

2. **Wisdom** *is* the ability of the believer to apply the knowledge of God to our everyday life.

3. The **wisdom** of God can only come through the Word of God.

IV. **TO GET DIRECTION**

A. **Psalm 119:130** (NIV) – "The unfolding of your words gives light; it gives understanding to the simple."

B. **Psalm 37:25** (NIV) – "I was young and now I am old, yet I have never seen the righteous forsaken or their children begging bread."

C. **Psalm 119:99** (NIV) – "I have more insight than all my teachers, for I meditate on your statutes."

D. **Psalm 119:105** (NLT) – "Your word is a lamp to guide my feet and a light for my path."

E. **Psalm 119:133** (NLT) – "Guide my steps by your word, so I will not be overcome by evil."

F. **Proverbs 3:5-6** (KJV) – "**Trust** in the Lord with all your heart, and lean not on your own understanding; in all thy ways acknowledge him, and he shall direct thy paths."

1. **Trust** in the Lord.

2. **Trust** in the Lord with all your heart.

3. **Trust** in the Lord with all your heart and lean not on your own understanding.

4. **Trust** in the Lord with all your heart and lean not on your own understanding; acknowledge all His ways, and He shall direct your paths.

V.   **TO BUILD OUR FAITH**

    A. **Hebrews 11:3** Young's Literal Translation (YLT) – "By faith we understand the ages to have been prepared by a saying of God, in regard to the things seen not having come out of things appearing."

    B. **Hebrews 11:6** (YLT) – "And apart from faith it is impossible to please well, for it behoveth him who is coming to God to believe that He is, and to those seeking Him He becometh a rewarder."

    C. **Romans 10:17** New King James Version (NKJV) – "So then faith *comes* by hearing, and hearing by **the word of God.**"

        1. The Word of God is a "faith builder."

        2. Increase your intake of the Word to increase your faith level.

        3. The Word of God builds our faith in God and His Word.

        4. Faith in God comes from having faith in His Word.

VI.   **TRANSFORMED LIFE**

    A. **Romans 12:1-2** (NKJV) – "I beseech you therefore, brethren, by the mercies of God, that you present your bodies a living sacrifice, holy, acceptable to God, which *is* your reasonable service. And **do not be conformed** to this world, but be transformed by the **renewing of your mind**, that you may prove what *is* that good and acceptable and perfect will of God."

        1. The Word of God has the ability to **renew our minds** to conform to the will of God.

        2. The Word of God converts the soul.

    B. **2 Corinthians 3:18** God's Word Translation (GWT) – "As all of us reflect the

Lord's glory with faces that are not covered with veils, we are being changed into his image with ever-increasing glory. This comes from the Lord, who is the Spirit."

C. **Acts 4:13** (NIV) – "When they saw the courage of Peter and John and realized that they were unschooled, ordinary men, they were astonished and they took note that these men had been with Jesus."

VII. TO OBTAIN KNOWLEDGE OF GOD

A. **Hosea 4:1** (NIV) – "Hear the word of the Lord, you Israelites, because the Lord has a charge to bring against you who live in the land: 'There is no faithfulness, no love, no acknowledgment of God in the land.'"

    1. Lack of knowledge of the Word of God leads to no acknowledgment of God in the land.

B. **Hosea 6:6** (NIV) – "For I desire mercy, not sacrifice, and acknowledgment of God rather than burnt offerings."

C. **Jeremiah 9:23-24** (NIV) – "This is what the Lord says: 'Let not the wise boast of their wisdom or the strong boast of their strength or the rich boast of their riches, but let the one who boasts boast about this: that they have the understanding to know me, that I am the Lord, who exercises kindness, justice and righteousness on earth, for in these I delight,' declares the Lord."

D. **Jeremiah 3:15** (NLT) – "And I will give you shepherds after my own heart, who will guide you with knowledge and understanding."

    1. The Word of God gives us knowledge and understanding.

    2. It is our responsibility to operate in the wisdom of God.

VIII. TO PREACH TO OTHERS

A. **1 Peter 3:15** (NIV) – "But in your hearts revere Christ as Lord. Always be prepared to give an answer to everyone who asks you to give the reason for the hope that you have. But do this with gentleness and respect."

B. **2 Timothy 4:2** (NKJV) – "Preach the word! Be ready in season and out of season. Convince, rebuke, exhort, with all longsuffering and teaching."

    1. **2 Timothy 4:2** (AMP) – "Whether the opportunity seems to be favorable or unfavorable."

2. Literally, the Greek text says, whether it is a good season or a bad season. We need to be instant.

3. The word *instant* comes from the Greek number 2186 *Ephistemi* which literally means to stand upon, in an active and upright position.

4. Stand upon the Word of God whether things are going well or things are going bad.

5. Stay grounded during your times of tribulations.

6. The Word of God must be preached when times are bad.

7. The Word of God must be preached when times are good.

SCRIPTURE MEMORY VERSE

John 15:7 (NKJV) – *"If you abide in Me, and My words abide in you, you will ask what you desire, and it shall be done for you."*

HOW TO STUDY THE WORD OF GOD

Introduction: Many believers desire to study the Word but have no idea how to study it. This lesson will provide practical ways to study the Word of God.

2 Timothy 2:15 (NIV) – "Do your best to present yourself to God as one approved, a worker who does not need to be ashamed and who correctly handles the word of truth."

I. Set aside a time to study.

    A. Design a specific area to study the Word of God.

    B. Pray about what to study.

        1. Select a small book first.

            a. First John, 2 John and 3 John are a great starting place.

        2. Give yourself four to five weeks to complete your study.

    C. Pray for understanding

        1. **Psalm 119:130** (KJV) – "The entrance of thy words giveth light; it giveth understanding unto the simple."

        2. **Psalm 119:130** (NIV) – "The unfolding of your words gives light; it gives understanding to the simple."

        3. **Psalm 119:130** (NLT) – "The teaching of your word gives light, so even the simple can understand."

            a. **Entrance** (Hebrew) *pethach* means opening, unfolding, entrance, doorway.

            b. **Words** (Hebrew) *dabar* means speech, word, speaking, thing. **Light** (Hebrew) *owr* means to give light, shine (of sun, moon and stars), to illumine, light up, cause to shine, shine, to kindle, light (candle, wood), lighten (of the eyes, his law, etc.).

            c. **Understanding** (Hebrew) *bene* means to cause to understand, give understanding, teach.

   d. **Simple** (Hebrew) *peth-ee'* - means simple, foolish, open-minded.

  4. **2 Timothy 3:16** (NIV) – "All Scripture is **God-breathed** and is **useful for teaching, rebuking, correcting** and **training in righteousness.**"

- God-breathed

- Useful for teaching

- Rebuking

- Correcting and training in righteousness

 D. Dissect a verse, chapter or book.

  1. **Seek understanding.**

  2. **Hebrews 4:12** (AMP) – "For the Word that God speaks is alive and full of power [making it active, operative, energizing, and effective]; it is sharper than any two-edged sword, penetrating to the dividing line of the breath of life (soul) and [the immortal] spirit, and of joints and marrow [of the deepest parts of our nature], exposing and sifting and analyzing and judging the very thoughts and purposes of the heart."

2. Word - saying or the utterance of God

3. Quick - alive and living, active

4. Powerful – active, working and energizing

5. Sharper - to cut, penetrating and convicting

6. Two-edged sword - *pistomos* means having a double mouth as a river.

7. Piercing - to go through.

8. Asunder - separate, rend and apart.

9. Discerner - to judge, to sift and analyze the intents and thoughts of the heart.

3. **Hebrews 4:12** (NLT) – "For the word of God is alive and powerful. It is sharper than the sharpest two-edged sword, cutting between soul and spirit, between joint and marrow. It exposes our innermost thoughts and desires."

   - The word of God is alive and powerful.

   - It is sharper than the sharpest two- edged sword.

   - Cutting between soul and spirit

   - Between joint and marrow

   - It exposes our innermost thoughts and desires.

1. The Word of God is full of life, always working.

2. The Word of God is a judge of the heart, thoughts and desires.

E. Use the right Bible study tools.

F. Apply the Word of God.

1. **Luke 11:28** (NLT) – "Jesus replied, 'But even more blessed are all who **hear the word of God** and **put it into practice.'**"

   - **Blessed are all who**

   - **Hear the Word of God**

   a. **Hear** (Greek) *akouo* means

2. **To** be endowed with the faculty of hearing, not deaf .

3. **To** hear, to attend to, consider what is or has been said .

4. **To** understand, perceive the sense of what is said .

5. **To** hear something.

6. **To** perceive by the ear what is announced in one's presence **To** get by hearing, learn .

7. A thing comes to one's ears, to find out, and learn.

8. **To** give ear to a teaching or a teacher.

9. **To** comprehend and to understand.

   • **Put it into practice**

      a. **Practice** is the act of rehearsing a behavior over and over, or engaging in an activity again and again, for the purpose of improving or mastering it, as in **the phrase "practice makes perfect."**

10. "Hear the Word of God and keep it."

11. **Luke 8:21** (NLT) - "Jesus replied, 'My mother and my brothers are all those who **hear** God's word and **obey** it.'"

   • Hear God's Word.

   • Obey it.

12. The true brothers and sisters in the body of Christ are they that do the will of God.

SCRIPTURE MEMORY VERSE

John 15:7 (NKJV) – *"If you abide in Me, and My words abide in you, you will ask what you desire, and it shall be done for you."*

THE INTEGRITY OF GOD'S WORD

Introduction: The Bible was written over a period of eighteen hundred years by forty human authors, on three continents and in three languages—Hebrew, Aramaic and Greek. Each author tells the same story. Even though the Bible is a best-seller, studies have shown that many Christians are biblically illiterate. If we value, esteem and treasure the Word we will have confidence in it. We will live it and apply it to our lives every day. The Bible consists of sixty-six books and was written by different people from all walks of life: farmers, shepherds, tentmakers, priests, teachers and preachers.

I. **The integrity of God's Word**

    A.   **John 1:1-2** (KJV) – "In the beginning was the word, and word was with God and the word was God, the same was in the beginning with God."

    B.   **Psalm 12:6-7** (KJV) – "The words of the Lord are pure words as silver tried in a furnace of earth, purified seven times. Thou shalt keep them O Lord, Thou shalt preserve them from this generation for ever."

        "God's Word is pure."

        "God's Word has no impurities."

    C.   When something has integrity it means it is **convincing, believable, dependable and trustworthy, and you can count on it.**

    D.   **Integrity** = honesty and soundness

    E.   God's integrity comes from God's Word.

    F.   **Psalm 119:89** (KJV) - "Forever, O Lord, thy word is settled in heaven."

II. **The integrity of God's Word means it has value, it is what it says it is, it will be fulfilled, and it has power for your life.**

    A.   The logos (written word) is a photocopy of what God has already used to release His faith on earth.

    B.   **Joshua 8:32** (KJV) – "And he wrote there upon the stones a copy of the law of Moses, which he wrote in the presence of the children of Israel."

C.   **Exodus 31:18** (KJV) – "Written with the finger of God."

D.   **Isaiah 55:10-11** (KJV) – "For as the rain cometh down, and the snow from heaven, and returneth not thither, but watereth the earth, and maketh it bring forth and bud, that it may give seed to the sower, and bread to the eater: So shall my word be that goeth forth out of my mouth: it shall not return unto me void, but it shall accomplish that which I please, and it shall prosper in the thing whereto I sent it."

E.   God's Word is a photocopy (fax copy) of God's original Word in heaven that He has sent to earth for the saints to live by as kingdom of God principles.

F.   **Proverbs 30:5-6** (KJV) – "Every word of God is pure: he is a shield unto them that put their trust in him. Add thou not unto his words, lest he reprove thee and thou be found a liar."

III.   **The Bible is God-breathed or God-inspired.**

A.   **Hebrews 11:3, Psalm 33:6, 9** - God releases His faith through His own Word.

   1.   God releases His ability and power through His Word.

   2.   The Word of God is eternal because God is eternal.

   3.   The Word of God is a performer and a producer.

B.   **Psalm 119:162** (KJV) – "I rejoice at thy word, as one that findeth great spoil."

C.   **Matthew 24:35** (KJV) – "Heaven and earth shall pass away, but my words shall not pass away."

D.   **2 Timothy 3:16** (KJV) – "All Scripture is given by **inspiration of God,** and is profitable for doctrine, for reproof, for correction, for instruction in righteousness."

E.   **2 Timothy 3:16-17** (NLT)

   1.   Provides sound doctrine.

   2.   **Reproof** means conviction and evidence.

   3.   **Correction** means a straightening up again, reformation.

   4.   **Instruction** means tutorage, education or training, chastening, chastisement and nurture.

F.   **Inspiration** means God-breathed, inspiration of God, inspiration by God.

G.   God breathed out the Scripture, or God produced the Scripture, as He did creation. **Psalm 33:6 - "By the word of the Lord"** were the heavens made; and all host of them by **the breath of his mouth."**

   1.   God created the heavens and the earth with His Word.

H.   **Job 32:8** (KJV) – "But there is **a spirit in man:** and **the inspiration** of the Almighty **giveth them understanding."**

I.   **Profitable** means useful, beneficial and helpful.

J.   **2 Peter 1:20, 21** (NKJV) – "Knowing this first, that no prophecy of Scripture is of any private interpretation **(explanation)**, for prophecy never came by the will of man, **but holy men of God spoke as they were moved by the Holy Spirit."**

IV.   **When we see the Scripture as inspired by God:**

A.   It produces the power and ability of God in our lives.

B.   **Ephesians 3:20** (KJV) – "Now unto him that is able to do exceeding abundantly above all that we ask or think, according to the power that worketh in us."

   1.   **God is able...**

      a.   **Able** (*dunamai*) means to be able, have power whether by virtue of one's own ability and resources, or of a state of mind, or through favorable circumstances, or by permission of law or custom. To be able to do something or to be capable, strong and powerful.

      b.   **To do exceeding abundantly above all that we ask or think.**

      c.   **According to the power that worketh in us.**

   2.   The ability of God is in His Word.

   3.   The Word of God is the ability of God.

   4.   God's Word has the ability to accomplish anything He wants to accomplish.

C.   **Luke 4:36** (KJV) – "And they were all amazed, and spake among themselves, saying, What a word is this! For with authority and power he commandeth the unclean spirits, and they come out."

D.   The Word of God produces the peace of God in our lives.

E.   God and His Word produce faith in our lives by hearing it. **Romans 10:17**.

F.   **Isaiah 40:8** (KJV) – "The grass withereth, the flower fadeth: but the word of our God shall stand for ever."

G.   **1 Peter 1:25** (KJV) – "But the word of the Lord endureth forever. And this is the Word which by the gospel is preached unto you."

SCRIPTURE MEMORY VERSE

John 15:7 (NKJV) – *"If you abide in Me, and My words abide in you, you will ask what you desire, and it shall be done for you."*

ABIDING IN THE WORD OF GOD

Introduction: The important thing in this time is that we would be people of God's Word. That we would let the Word of God dwell in us, live in us, and that we would live by it. Your Word level will determine your faith level (Romans 10:17). Little word, little faith. Abiding in the Word produces an effective prayer life.

I.   **Abiding in the Word of God**

    A.   **John 15:7** (NKJV) – "If you abide in Me, and My words abide in you, you will ask what you desire, and it shall be done for you."

    B.   **John 15:7** (LNT) – "**But if you** stay in me and obey my commands, you may ask any request you like, and **it will be granted!**"

        1.   John 15:7 is the key to getting our prayers answered.

        2.   **"Abiding" means vital, united relationship where you are drawing your life strength from Him.** To dwell, continue, stay, sojourn, rest in or upon. It is being set and fixed and remaining there, continuing on and on in a fixed state, condition or being.

        3.   Jesus used the analogy of a branch connected to a vine. The vine goes deep into the soil, **the roots pull up the nutrients,** they go into the branches, and branches bear the leaves and fruit.

        4.   **The vine is** always **nourishing the branch,** always sending its **life-giving food** and **drink to the branch.**

        5.   "**Abide in me,** and I in you. As the branch cannot bear fruit of itself, except it abide in the vine; no more can ye except ye abide in me." **NOTE:** The unattached branch is "out" and off by itself; it is not abiding in the vine and not attached. It is "of itself."

        6.   The two keys to getting your prayers answered are: (1) **to abide in Jesus** and (2) **to have His Word abide in you.**

        7.   We must let the Word dwell in our spirits. The choice is up to you to let the Word dwell in your heart.

        8.   "Let the word of Christ dwell in you richly in all wisdom; teaching and admonishing one another in psalms and hymns and spiritual songs, singing with grace in your hearts to the Lord" (**Colossians 3:17**).

        9.   Letting the Word of God dwell in us richly will lead us to the wisdom of God.

10.   **Dwell** (*enoikeito*) means to be at home; to abide or live within.

11.   Abiding in the Word of God produces an effective prayer life in the believer.

12.   The abiding Word of God overcomes the wicked one.

II.   **To have more freedom you need more of the Word.**

    A.   **John 8:31, 32, 36** - "If you abide in My word, you are My disciples indeed. And you shall know the truth, and the truth shall make you free. . .Therefore if the Son makes you free, you shall be free indeed."

    B.   If you don't have fuel you won't have fire.

III.   **The different ways to abide in the Word.**

    A.   To the degree you value and esteem the integrity of the Word is the degree you will be in the Word – **Joshua 1:8, Psalm 119:9-11**.

        1.   When you hear the Word you retain **ten percent.**

        2.   When you read the Word you retain **twenty-five percent.**

        3.   When you study the Word you retain **fifty percent.**

        4.   When you memorize the Word you retain **one hundred percent.**

        5.   When you meditate on the Word you retain **one hundred percent.**

- **Hear** the Word

James 1:22-25 (KJV) – "But be ye doers of the word, and not hearers only, deceiving your own selves. For if any be a hearer of the word, and not a doer, he is like unto a man beholding his natural face in a glass: For he beholdeth himself, and goeth his way, and straightway forgetteth what manner of man he was."

- **Read** the Word

- **Study** the Word

- **Memorize** the Word

- **Apply** the Word

- **Meditate** upon the Word

SCRIPTURE MEMORY VERSE

John 15:7 (NKJV) – *"If you abide in Me, and My words abide in you, you will ask what you desire, and it shall be done for you."*

KEYS TO THE MANIFESTATION OF THE WORD OF GOD IN YOUR LIFE

Introduction: Many believers share a knowledge of the Word of God, but they do not know how to get the Word to manifest in their lives. There are several keys to getting the Word to manifest in your life: hearing it, reading it, studying it, memorizing it and meditating upon it. This will guarantee manifestation of the Word in your life.

Mark 4:20 (NIV) – "Others, like seed sown on good soil, **hear the word, accept it, and produce a crop**—some thirty, some sixty, some a hundred times what was sown."

I.   HEARING THE WORD OF GOD

A. **Romans 10:17** (KJV) – "So then faith cometh by hearing, and hearing by the word of God."

1.   Notice the process of obtaining faith.

2.   Hearing—and hearing the Word of God.

   a.   **Hearing** – a sincere desire to receive and understand the message.

   b.   An attitude of aroused attention.

3.   Faith cometh:

   a.   **Faith** – assurance, belief, believe, reliance for salvation in Christ, truth itself, have confidence and trust.

   b.   **Cometh** – appear, bring, enter, go, grow, to come.

4.   Faith comes from hearing one thing, and that's the Word of God.

5.   You cannot have faith for something if you do not hear the Word of God on it.

6.   Faith in God is produced by hearing the Word of God.

B. **James 1:22** (KJV) – "But be ye doers of the word, and not hearers only, deceiving your own selves."

1.   **Be ye doers of the Word.**

   a.   **Doers** (Greek, *poyaytace*) means a producer and performer of the Word of God.

b. One who obeys or fulfills the law.

2. Hearers of the Word only bring on deception.

C. The particular passage "hear the Word of the Lord" occurs thirty-two times in the NIV and twenty-eight times in the NASB.

D. **Hearing the Word of God has the ability to change our thinking.**

1. At Stanford University a study was conducted concerning hearing. It was discovered that in order to form an opinion a person has to hear it **seven times.** If a person has the wrong opinion already on a particular subject, then a person needs to hear the right opinion **eleven times** in order to eradicate the wrong opinion, with an even further **seven hearing times** to secure it. It takes a total of **eighteen times.**

2. **Luke 8:21** (NKJV) – "But He answered and said to them, 'My mother and My brothers are these who **hear** the word of God and **do it.**'"

    a. Hear the Word God.

    b. Do it (obey it).

3. Jesus said that His brethren are those who hear the Word of God and do it.

4. We must train our ears to hear the Word of God.

5. How we hear is the key to obtaining the blessing of God through the Word of God.

6. We must train our ears to understand the Word of God.

7. **Deuteronomy 30:10-14** (NIV) – "If you obey the Lord your God and keep his commands and decrees that are written in this Book of the Law and turn to the Lord your God with all your heart and with all your soul. Now what I am commanding you today is not too difficult for you or beyond your reach. It is not up in heaven, so that you have to ask, 'Who will ascend into heaven to get it and proclaim it to us so we may obey it?' Nor is it beyond the sea, so that you have to ask, 'Who will cross the sea to get it and proclaim it to us so we may obey it?' No, the word is very near you; it is in your mouth and in your heart so you may obey it."

8. **Proverbs 4:20-22** (KJV) – "My son, attend to my words; incline thine ear unto my sayings. Let them not depart from thine eyes; keep them in the midst of thine heart. For they are life unto those that find them, and health to all their flesh."

    1. **Attend** (*Kawshab*) - to hear, be attentive, heed, incline of ears, attend of ears, hearken, pay attention, give attention.

2. **Words** (*daw baw*) - speech, speaking, saying, utterance, commandment.

3. **Incline** (*naw taw*) - to stretch out, bend, bow.

4. **Ear** (*ozen*) - receiver of divine revelation.

5. **Eyes** (*ainwn*) - as showing mental qualities, physical eye, of mental and spiritual faculties.

6. **Keep** (*shawmar*) - to keep guard and observe.

7. **Midst** - in the middle.

8. **Heart** (*lay bawb*) -inner man, a seat of emotions, passions, understanding, mind; soul, heart of man.

9. **Life** (*Khahee*) -living, alive, active of man.

10. **Health** -medicine, healing, cure, sound of mind.

11. **Flesh** - of the body.

E. **Proverbs 4:20-22** gives us instructions on how to take God's Word into our inner man.

    •   **Attend to** the Word of God.

    •   **Incline** your ear unto the sayings of God.

    •   Let God's Word **not depart** from your eyes.

    •   **Keep it** in the midst of your heart.

F. **Matthew 13:13-17** is the opposite of **Proverbs 4:20-22**.

> "Therefore speak I to them in parables: because they seeing see not; and hearing they hear not, neither do they understand. And in them is fulfilled the prophecy of Esaias, which saith, By hearing ye shall hear, and shall not understand; and seeing ye shall see, and shall not perceive: For this people's heart is waxed gross, and their ears are dull of hearing, and their eyes they have closed; lest at any time they should see with their eyes and hear with their ears, and should understand with their heart, and should be converted, and I should heal them. But blessed are your eyes, for they see: and your ears, for they hear. For verily I say unto you, That many prophets and righteous men have desired to see those things which ye see, and have not seen them; and to hear those things which ye hear, and have not heard them."

9. **Luke 11: 28** (KJV) – "But he said, Yea rather, **blessed** are **they that hear the word of God**, and **keep it**."

   a. Blessed

   b. They that hear the word of God

   c. Keep it

10. **Luke 11:28** (LNT) – "Jesus replied, 'But even more blessed are all who hear the word of God and **put it into practice.**'"

11. **Matthew 13:23** (NIV) – "But the seed falling on **good soil** refers to someone who **hears the word** and **understands it**. This is the one who **produces a crop**, **yielding a hundred**, **sixty** or **thirty times** what was **sown**."

    • Good soil

    • Hears the Word

    • Understands it

    • Produces a crop

    • Yielding a hundred

    • Sixty

    • Thirty times

    • Sown

12. **Matthew 15:10** – *"Hear and understand."*

13. **"The Word of God should produce fruit in your life."**

G. **Luke 8:11-15** (KJV) – "Now the parable is this: The seed is the word of God. Those by the wayside are the ones **who hear;** then the devil comes and takes away the word out of their hearts, lest they should believe and be saved. But the ones on the rock *are those* who, when **they hear**, receive the word with joy; and these have no root, who believe for a while and in time of temptation fall away. Now the ones *that* fell among thorns are those who, when **they have heard**, go out and are choked with cares, riches, and pleasures of life, and bring no fruit to maturity. But the ones *that* fell on the good ground are those who, **having heard** the word with a noble and good heart, keep *it* and bear fruit with patience."

1. The **seed** is the Word of God.

2. **Seed** (*sproos*) - a saving seed (used in sowing); seed sown.

3. Hear or heard is mentioned four times in the above passage of Scripture.

4. Hear (*akoo-o*) - to be endowed with the faculty of hearing, to get by hearing, learn. A thing to one's ears, to find out, learn to give ear to, a teaching or a teacher, to comprehend or to understand.

H. **Mark 4:14-20** (KJV) – "The sower soweth the word. And these are they by the way side, where the word is sown; but when **they have heard**, Satan cometh immediately, and taketh away the word that was sown in their hearts. And these are they likewise which are sown on stony ground; who, when **they have heard the word,** immediately receive it with gladness; And have no root in themselves, and so endure but for a time: afterward, when affliction or persecution ariseth for the word's sake, immediately they are offended. And these are they which are sown among thorns; **such as hear the word**, And the cares of this world, and the deceitfulness of riches, and the lusts of other things entering in, choke the word, and it becometh unfruitful. And these are they which are sown on good ground; **such as hear the word**, and receive it, and bring forth fruit, some thirtyfold, some sixty, and some an hundred."

1. "They have heard," "they have heard the word" or "such as hear the word" is mentioned four times in the above passage.

2. We hear the Word of God, receive the Word of God and bring forth fruit.

II. THE BLESSING OF READING THE WORD OF GOD

A. **Revelation 1:3** (KJV) – "Blessed is he that readeth, and they that hear the words of this prophecy, and keep those things which are written therein: for the time is at hand."

- **Blessed** is he that **readeth.**

    a. **Blessed** (Greek, *makarios*) - blessed, happy.

    b. **Readeth** (Greek, *anaginoskoto*) - distinguish between, to recognize, to know accurately, to acknowledge and to read.

- They that **hear** the **words** of this **prophecy.**

    a. **Hear** (Greek, *akouo*) - to give ear to a teaching or a teacher and to comprehend, to understand, to perceive the sense of what is said.

    b. **Words** (Greek, *logos*) -the sayings of God, the act of speaking.

    c. **Prophecy** (Greek, *propheteia*) -of the endowment and speech of the Christian teachers called prophets. The gifts and utterances of these prophets, especially of the predictions of the works of which, set apart to teach the gospel, will accomplish for the kingdom of Christ.

- **Keep** those things which are written therein.

    a. **Keep** (Greek, *tereo*) = to attend to carefully, take care of, to guard, to keep one in the state in which he is, to observe and to **reserve** , to undergo something.

B. **Benefits from reading the Word of God**

1. The Lord reveals Himself to us.

2. The Lord reveals His will for our lives.

3. The Lord opens our spiritual eyes by giving the spirit of discernment.

4. God speaks to us through His Word.

5. Reading the Word of God is an opportunity to get to know the ways and thoughts of God.

6. The ways of God and the thoughts of God come from the Word of God.

7. Learning the things of God

8. **Proverbs 22:17-22** (NIV) – "Pay attention and turn your ear to the sayings of the wise; apply your heart to what I teach, for it is pleasing when you keep them in your heart and have all of them ready on your lips. So that your trust may be in the Lord, I teach you today, even you. Have I not written thirty sayings for you, sayings of counsel and knowledge, teaching you to be honest and to speak the truth, so that you bring back truthful reports to those you serve?"

9. The revealed will of God is known.

10. **Isaiah 34:16** (YLT) – "Seek out of the book of Jehovah, and read, One of these hath not been lacking, none hath missed its companion, for My mouth—it hath commanded, and His spirit—He hath gathered them."

11. **1 Samuel 3:21** (NIV) – **"The Lord continued to appear at Shiloh, and there he revealed himself to Samuel through his word."**

- The Lord continued to appear at Shiloh.

- There He revealed Himself to Samuel through His Word.

C. **1 Timothy 4:13** (KJV) – "Till I come, give attendance to reading, to exhortation, to doctrine."

D. **1 Timothy 4:13** (NIV) – "Until I come, devote yourself to the public reading of scripture, to preaching and to teaching."

"PUBLIC OR PRIVATE READING"

a. **Attendance** (Greek, *prosecho*) -to apply oneself to, attach oneself to, hold or cleave, to a person or a thing, to be given or addicted to, to devote thought and effort to.

b. **Reading** (Greek, *anagnosis*) - knowing, a knowing again, owning, reading.

c. **Exhortation** (Greek, *paraklesis*) -a calling near, summons (especially for help), exhortation, admonition, encouragement, consolation, comfort, solace; that which affords comfort or refreshment.

d. **Doctrine** (Greek, *didaskalia*) -teaching, instruction, teaching, that which is taught, doctrine, teachings, precepts.

"ATTENDANCE"

- **To reading**

- **To exhortation**

- **To doctrine**

2. When we read the Word of God we are reading the *will of God*.

3. God's Word is His will for our lives.

III. STUDYING THE WORD OF GOD

A. "Devoted himself to study and observance of the law of the word to teaching its decrees and laws in Israel."

B. **2 Timothy 2:15** (KJV) – "Study to shew thyself approved unto God, a workman that needeth not to be ashamed, rightly dividing the word of truth."

"Study to shew thyself approved unto God."

C. **2 Timothy 2:15** (AMP) – "**Study** and be eager and do your utmost to present yourself to God **approved** (tested by trial), a workman who has no cause to be ashamed, correctly analyzing and accurately dividing [rightly handling and skillfully teaching] the Word of Truth."

    a. **Study** (Greek, *spoudazo*) - to exert oneself, endeavor, give diligence, to labor and make haste, be earnest or diligent.

    b. **Study** - to set your heart upon, be diligent, hurry, rush, seek the approval of God.

    c. **Study** - the mental effort, put forth in an attempt to add to one's store of knowledge and one's ability to use that knowledge in an effective way.

1. **Study** is the "first" thing a person must do in order to rightly divide the word of truth.

    d. **Approved** (Greek, *dokimos*) = accepted, pleasing, acceptable and tried. The ancient world had no banking system as we know it today and no paper money. All money was made from metal, heated until liquid, poured into moulds and allowed to cool. When the coins were cooled, it was necessary to smooth off the uneven edges. The coins were comparatively soft, and of course many people shaved them closely. In one century more than eighty laws were passed in Athens to stop the practice of shaving down the coins then in circulation. But some money-changers were men of integrity, who would accept no counterfeit money. They were men of honour who put only genuine full-weighted money into circulation. Such men were called "*dokimos*" or "*approved*" (Donald Barnhouse).

    e. A workman that needeth not to be ashamed

    f. **Workman** (Greek, *ergates*) = one who does, a worker, workman, laborer, perpetrator

    g. **Ashamed** (Greek, *anepaischuntos*) = having no cause to be ashamed

    h. Rightly dividing the word of truth

    i. **Rightly** (Greek, *orthotomeo*) = to cut straight, to cut straight ways; to proceed on straight paths, hold a straight course, equivalent to doing right; to make straight and smooth, to handle aright, to teach the truth directly and correctly.

  j. **Orthos** = perfectly right or perfectly straight

  k. To teach the truth directly and correctly

  l. **Temno** = to cut

  m. Putting these two words together in the *orthotomounta*, translated rightly dividing in the KJV, literally means a perfect, right cutting.

  n. **Word** (Greek, *logos*) = a word, uttered by a living voice, embodies a conception or idea, what someone has said, a word, the sayings of God; to decree, mandate or order.

  o. **Truth** (Greek, *aletheia*) = of a truth, in reality, in fact, certainly

OTHER TRANSLATIONS:

- Handling aright the word of truth (ASV)

- Rightly handling the Word of truth (ESV)

- One who correctly teaches the message of God's truth (GNB)

- Handling the Word of truth with precision (ISV)

D. **Acts 17:11** (KJV) – "These were more **noble** than those in Thessalonica, in that they **received** the **word** with all readiness of mind, and searched the scriptures daily, whether those things were so."

  a. **Noble** (Greek, *eugenes*) = well born, of a noble family, noble minded

  b. **Received** (Greek, *dechomaito*) = receive favorably, give ear to, embrace, make one's own, approve, not to reject

  c. **Word** (Greek, *logos*) = word, uttered by a living voice, speech, saying, embodies a conception or idea.

  d. **Readiness of mind** (Greek, *prothumia*) = zeal, spirit, eagerness, inclination, a readiness of mind

  e. **Searched** (Greek, *anakrinoto*) = investigate, examine, enquire into, scrutinize, sift, question

  f. Scriptures

IV. THE BLESSING OF MEMORIZING THE WORD OF GOD

A. Memorize:

- To commit to memory

- Learn by heart

- The process of committing something to memory

B. Memorizing the Word of God allows the Word of God to saturate our hearts.

C. **Psalm 119:9-11** (KJV) – "Wherewithal shall a young man cleanse his way? by taking heed thereto according to thy word. With my whole heart have I sought thee: O let me not wander from thy commandments. Thy word have I hid in mine heart, that I might not sin against thee."

D. **Deuteronomy 11:13** (KJV) – "And it shall come to pass, if ye shall hearken diligently unto my commandments which I command you this day, to love the Lord your God, and to serve him with all your heart and with all your soul."

E. **Keys to memorizing the Word of God**

- Identify verses that deal with your current situation.

- Read those verses or that verse out loud over and over.

- Memorize all or part of it.

- Memorize the Word day and night.

- Observe it.

- Apply it daily.

V. MEDITATE UPON THE WORD OF GOD

A. **Joshua 1:8** (KJV) – "This book of the law shall not depart out of thy mouth;

but thou shalt meditate therein day and night, that thou mayest observe to do according to all that is written therein: for then thou shalt make thy way prosperous, and then thou shalt have good success."

1. **This book of the law shall not depart out of thy mouth.**

      a. Law - instruction, guidance, priestly instruction

2. **Meditate therein day and night.**

      a. Meditate - to muse over, ponder, to plan in the mind, to purpose over, intend.

      b. Muse - ponder, to weigh in the mind, to think about, reflect on, to think about, especially quietly, soberly and deeply.

      c. Speak the Word of God over and over.

      d. **The Greek word implies to revolve something in the mind and is also translated to imagine a word picture.**

      e. **Repetition** -the action of repeating something.

      f. The act or process or an instance of repeating or being repeated.

3. **Observe to do according to all that is written therein.**

      a. **Observe** (Hebrew, shaw-mar') -to keep, guard, keep watch and ward, protect, save life; to keep, retain, treasure up (in memory).

      a. **To do** (Hebrew ,aw-saw') -to do, fashion, accomplish, make and to do, work, make, produce.

4. **Thou shalt make thy way prosperous.**

      a. **Prosperous** (Hebrew, tsaw-lay'-akh) = to advance, prosper, make progress, succeed, be profitable and (Qal) to prosper, to make prosperous, bring to successful issue, cause to and prosper to show or experience prosperity.

5. **Thou shalt have good success.**

      a. **Success** (Hebrew, saw-kal') = prosper, have success and to cause to prosper

B. **Results of meditating upon the Word of God**

Psalm 1:1-3 (KJV) – "Blessed is the man that walketh not in the counsel of the ungodly, nor standeth in the way of sinners, nor sitteth in the seat of the scornful. But his delight is in the law of the Lord; and in his law doth he meditate day and night. And he shall be like a tree planted by the rivers of water, that bringeth forth his fruit in his season; his leaf also shall not wither; and whatsoever he doeth shall prosper."

    1. Delight

2. The law of the Lord

3. Meditate

4. A tree planted by the rivers of water

5. Bringeth forth his fruit

6. His season

7. His leaf shall not wither

8. Whatsoever he doeth shall prosper

C. Reasons why we should meditate upon the Word of God

- Psalm 119:148 (NIV) – "My eyes stay open through the watches of the night, that I may meditate on your promises."

- God commanded us to.

- It renews our minds.

- It allows God to speak to us through His Word.

- It allows us to reflect and think about God.

- It is the key to living a successful life.

SCRIPTURE MEMORY VERSE

John 15:7 (NKJV) – "If you abide in Me, and My words abide in you, you will ask what you desire, and it shall be done for you."

PRAYING THE WORD OF GOD

Introduction: Many prayers go unanswered due to lack of knowledge and how to pray effectively. One way to guarantee results is to pray the Word of God that's applicable to your situation. This lesson will provide you with the knowledge of praying the Word of God to get results.

1 John 5:14,15 (KJV) - "Now this is the confidence that we have in Him, that if we ask anything according to His will, He hears us. And if we know that He hears us, whatever we ask, we know that we have the petitions that we have asked of Him."

I. Praying the Word of God will get your prayers answered. It may not be the way we want him to answer our prayers.

A. We must know and have confidence in God's Word.

Confidence = boldness, trust, confide in.

We must ask in Jesus' name.

John 16:23 (NIV) – "In that day you will no longer ask me anything. Very truly I tell you, my Father will give you whatever you ask in my name."

1. You must ask according to the will of God.

a. The will of God is found in the Word of God.

b. **John 15:7** (NIV) – "If you remain in me and my words remain in you, ask whatever you wish, and it will be done for you."

2. We must have confidence that God hears our prayers.

a. **Psalm 66:18-20** (NIV) – "If I had cherished sin in my heart, the Lord would not have listened; but God has surely listened and has heard my prayer. Praise be to God, who has not rejected my prayer or withheld his love from me!"

3. Be confident and expectant that you will receive God's response.

4. Confidence in the Word of God is confidence in God.

II. How Do You Know God's Will?

    A. First, it is by the Holy Spirit – John 14:26.

    B. The Holy Spirit helps our infirmities – Romans 8:26-28.

        1. The Holy Spirit is a helper in every area of our lives.

        2. The Holy Spirit intercedes for us when needed.

        3. The Holy Spirit will help us. He won't do it alone; we must participate.

        4. Infirmities = the inability to produce results.

    C. His Word – God's Word and His will are the same thing – John 15:7.

III. How to Pray the Word of God

    A. **2 Corinthians 13:1** – "By the mouth of two or three witnesses every word shall be established."

        1. Find a word or words that are applicable to your situation or your need.

        2. Meditate upon the Word of God and not the problem.

            Joshua 1:8- This book shall not depart from your mouth.

            - Meditate day and night.

            - Observe to do all that is written therein.

            - Make thy way prosperous.

            - Then thou shalt have good success.

        3. Thank God for the answer according to His Word.

        4. God's Word will never return to us void; it will always accomplish the thing He sends it to.

            a. **Isaiah 55:8-11** Young's Literal Translation (YLT) – "For not My thoughts [are] your thoughts, nor your ways My ways—an affirmation of Jehovah, for high have the heavens been above the earth, so high have been My ways above your ways, and My thoughts above your thoughts. For, as come down doth the shower, and the snow from the heavens, and thither returneth not, but hath watered the earth, and hath caused it to yield, and to spring up, and hath given seed to the sower, and bread to the eater, so is My word that goeth out of My mouth. It turneth not back unto Me empty, but hath done that which I desired, and prosperously effected that [for] which I sent it."

5. **Praying the Word of God will release the ability and power of God in your life.**

B. Ensure your heart is a good and honest heart.

Luke 8:15 (NIV) – "But the seed on good soil stands for those with a noble and good heart, who hear the word, retain it, and by persevering produce a crop." **Good ground – This is a heart that hears the Word, receives it and brings forth fruit; some thirtyfold, some sixty and some a hundred.**

IV. Now is the time to plant the Word of God in your heart.

D. Plant a word for now and a word for later – Psalm 119:9-11.

1. You will need the Word of God every day, and you will need the Word of God during a crisis.

SCRIPTURE MEMORY VERSE
1 John 5:14, 15 (NKJV) – *"Now this is the confidence that we have in Him, that if we ask anything according to His will, He hears us. And if we know that He hears us, whatever we ask, we know that we have the petitions that we have asked of Him."*

DAILY BIBLE DEVOTION

WEEK OF: _____

SUNDAY: Scripture text for the day: _____ Date: _____

What is God's word to me today?_____

What has God promised me? _____

What is God telling me to obey? _____

How can I apply this word to my life today? _____

MONDAY: Scripture text for the day: _____ Date: _____

What is God's word to me today? _____

What has God promised me? _____

What is God telling me to obey? _____

How can I apply this word to my life today? _____

TUESDAY: Scripture text for the day: _____ Date: _____

What is God's word to me today? _____

What has God promised me? _____

What is God telling me to obey? _____

How can I apply this word to my life today? _____

WEDNESDAY: Scripture text for the day: _____ Date: _____

What is God's word to me today? _____

What has God promised me? _____

What is God telling me to obey? _____

How can I apply this word to my life today? _____

THURSDAY: Scripture text for the day: _____ Date: _____

What is God's word to me today? _____

What has God promised me? _____

What is God telling me to obey? _____

How can I apply this word to my life today? _____

FRIDAY: Scripture text for the day: _____ Date: _____

What is God's word to me today? _____

What has God promised me? _____

What is God telling me to obey? _____

How can I apply this word to my life today? _____

SATURDAY: Scripture text for the day: _____ Date: _____

What is God's word to me today? _____

What has God promised me? _____

What is God telling me to obey? _____

How can I apply this word to my life today? _____

SCRIPTURE MEMORY VERSE

2 Timothy 2:15 – *"Study to shew thyself approved unto God, a workman that needeth not to be ashamed, rightly dividing the word of truth."*

HOW TO CONDUCT A CHAPTER ANALYSIS

Scripture text: _____ **Date:** _____

1. What is the main subject in the entire text?

2. Who are the main characters?

3. What does it say about God, Christ and the Holy Spirit?

4. What is the key verse in the entire chapter?

5. What is the main lesson in the text?

6. What promises are in the chapter?

7. What is the main commandment?

8. What can I learn from the chapter on what to do and what not to do?

9. How can I apply this chapter to my life?

SCRIPTURE MEMORY VERSE

2 Timothy 2:15 – *"Study to shew thyself approved unto God, a workman that needeth not to be ashamed, rightly dividing the word of truth."*

HOW TO OUTLINE A CHAPTER

Bible chapter:_____ **Date:** _____

Write a short summary of the main subject of the chapter.

What is the key verse in the chapter?

To whom is the chapter written?

OUTLINE THE CHAPTER:

Introduction:

Background:

SCRIPTURE MEMORY VERSE

2 Timothy 2:15 – *"Study to shew thyself approved unto God, a workman that needeth not to be ashamed, rightly dividing the word of truth."*

HOW TO CONDUCT A BOOK STUDY

Name of the book: _____ **Date read:** _____

1. Who is the author of the book?

2. Why was the book written?

3. To whom was the book written?

4. In what location was it written?

5. What was the main concern?

6. What did the writer instruct them to do?

7. How is it relevant to today's church?

8. What sin did he or she commit and confess?

9. What service did they provide to God?

10. Describe their relationship with God and their family.

11. How were their children? Good or bad?

12. What is the main lesson we can learn from their lives?

13. How can the church or an individual apply any of these things listed of the characters ?

SCRIPTURE MEMORY VERSE

2 Timothy 2:15 – *"Study to shew thyself approved unto God, a workman that needeth not to be ashamed, rightly dividing the word of truth."*

HOW TO STUDY A PROVERB

Proverb: _____   **Date:** _____

The book of Proverbs is written to gain wisdom.

1. In the book of Proverbs what is the principal thing?

2. What is a proverb?

3. What is wisdom?

4. What are we instructed not to do?

5. What are the commandments in Proverbs?

6. What is the main subject in Proverbs?

7. How can we apply Proverbs to our lives?

SCRIPTURE MEMORY VERSE

2 Timothy 2:15 – _"Study to shew thyself approved unto God, a workman that needeth not to be ashamed, rightly dividing the word of truth."_

BIBLE CHARACTER STUDY

Name of the character: _____

Scripture passage of the character: _____

1. List other scriptures regarding his/her life.

2. Give a brief summary of their childhood, their parents, family, occupation and education.

3. What are the good and bad character traits?

4. Describe their experience with God.

5. Who are the other characters involved with the main character(s)?

6. What can be learned from their lives?

SCRIPTURE MEMORY VERSE

2 Timothy 2:15 – *"Study to shew thyself approved unto God, a workman that needeth not to be ashamed, rightly dividing the word of truth."*

TOOLS FOR BIBLE STUDY

I.   **Tools for Bible Study**

    A. Book-by-book survey of the Bible

    B. Bible atlas

    C. Vine's or Strong's Bible concordance

    D. Vine's or Strong's Bible dictionary

    E. Different Bible commentary

    F. Different translations

    G. Lexicon

    H. Webster's dictionary

    I. Thompson Chain-Reference Bible

    J. Strong's Exhaustive Concordance

    K. Vine's Expository Dictionary

    L. Biblegateway.com

    M. Hebrew/Greek study Bible

SCRIPTURE MEMORY VERSE

2 Timothy 2:15 – *"Study to shew thyself approved unto God, a workman that needeth not to be ashamed, rightly dividing the word of truth."*

HOW TO DO A STUDY IN PSALMS

Passage: _____ **Date:** _____

1. To whom were the Psalms written?

2. Who wrote the Psalms?

3. What are the blessings of the Psalms?

4. How many promises are listed in the Psalms?

5. What are the commandments of the Psalms?

6. Is there any mention of Christ in the Psalms?

7. What is the main subject in the Psalms?

8. How can we apply the Psalms to our lives?

   9.

HOW TO STUDY THE PARABLES OF JESUS

Name of the parable: _____ **Date:** _____

Scripture text: _____

1. What is a parable?

2. Why did Jesus teach this parable?

3. Give a brief summary of the parable.

4. How does Jesus convey a spiritual thought from the parable?

5. What is the main subject of the parable?

6. How can the parable be applied to our lives?

SCRIPTURE MEMORY VERSE

2 Timothy 2:15 – *"Study to shew thyself approved unto God, a workman that needeth not to be ashamed, rightly dividing the word of truth."*

THE LIFE, MINISTRY AND TEACHING OF JESUS

Scripture text: _____ **Date:** _____

1. What does this passage say about Jesus' life?

2. What happened before Jesus could start His earthly ministry?

3. What are the Gospels?

4. How many parables did Jesus teach?

5. List the main points about His life.

6. Who were Jesus' enemies during His earthly ministry?

7. What was Jesus' earthly ministry?

8. What opposition did Jesus encounter during His ministry?

9. Where is it recorded that Jesus is the Son of God?

10. How many times was it recorded that Jesus taught and how many times did He preach, according to the Gospels?

11. What can we learn from His teaching of the Beatitudes?

12. How can we apply Jesus' teachings to our lives?

13. What can we learn from Jesus' prayer life?

14. What did Jesus teach His disciples to do?

15. What did Jesus say His house should be called?

SCRIPTURE MEMORY VERSE

Matthew 4: 23-25 – _"And Jesus went about all Galilee, teaching in their synagogues, and preaching the gospel of the kingdom, and healing all manner of sickness and all manner of disease among the people. And his fame went throughout all Syria: and they brought unto him all sick people that were taken with divers diseases and torments, and those which were possessed with devils, and those which were lunatic, and those that had the palsy; and he healed them. And there followed him great multitudes of people from Galilee, and from Decapolis, and from Jerusalem, and from Judaea, and from beyond Jordan."_

EFFECTIVE TIME MANAGEMENT

"To everything there is a season and a time to every purpose under the heaven."

"There is an opportune time to do things for everything on earth."

Ecclesiastes 3:1 (The Message Bible)

Introduction: The Bible uses the word *time* in **594 different places**. Every morning the Lord wakes us up, and He gives every person **86,400 seconds** to do whatever we want to do with them. This time can't be carried over to the next day. You can either use it or lose it. Benjamin Franklin said, "Time is what life is made of." When we give people or projects our time we are giving them a portion of our lives. People who value their lives use their time wisely. The quality of our lives will be influenced by the quality of our time management. Managing our time properly is the key to our future. If we don't manage our time, it will manage us. We need to manage our time more effectively, not just to make more money, but to pursue our God-given purpose for living. Time will come and go whether we do anything with it or not.

I. **Time is one thing we all have been given equally.**

"Teach us *to number our days* so we can **apply our lives to wisdom**. There is the wisdom of God that will show us His **path, direction** and **will**" (Psalm 90:12).

A. The better we use our time, the more time we seem to have. We all have the same twenty-four hours in a day; there are 7 days in our week, the same 365 days in our year. The only difference between us and the next person is how we utilize those hours, days, weeks and years.

   1. People who waste a lot of time never have enough time.

   2. Teddy Roosevelt said, "Nine-tenths of wisdom consists of being wise in time."

   3. Our time must be managed properly and wisely.

   4. We need to make the best of the time we have available. Remember: every day is important.

B. **We cannot deposit time not used for another day.**

   1. We cannot deposit twenty-four hours to be used later because there is no drawing tomorrow.

   2. You must live and use your today's deposit of time.

3. We either use it wisely or lose it foolishly, and when time is gone it is gone forever!

4. Time is not a promise; it is a gift.

5. People who get a lot done use their time wisely.

II. Ways we can use our time wisely

"And he said unto them, how is it that ye sought me? Wist ye not that **I must be about my Father's business?**" (Luke 2:49).

A. **At least ten percent of our time should go to God and His purposes.**

1. The thing that gives worth to our gifts of tithe, talent and time is the fact that these gifts cost us a portion of our lives.

2. When we give to God money, talent and time we are giving Him the value of the portion of our lives we used to be able to present the time, talent and money to Him.

3. We cannot use time or money in any better way than to give it to God's cause and glory.

III. Ways we can get the most out of our time

A. Manage your time from a "things to do" list.

1. Focus on the task of highest value first.

2. Tackle the most difficult or unpleasant task in your most productive hours.

3. Don't be consumed by detail and drudgery.

4. Be selective in what takes up your time.

5. Learn to say no to projects that take you away from your priorities.

6. Set realistic deadlines for completing key projects.

7. Eliminate self-made distractions. Minimize those imposed by others, such as unnecessary phone calls, visitors or visits, etc.

8. Learn to say no!

9. Keep a daily "things to do" list.

B. **Learn to delegate**

Delegation means to entrust your authority or functions to subordinates; to enlist persons to complete tasks that you would otherwise have undertaken yourself. It is accomplishing results through the efforts of others.

1. Do only what you alone can do.

2. Empower people, but check on them.

3. We don't have to do everything in order to have value in our lives.

4. Delegate tasks that others can do.

5. This will give you the ability to convey trust, inspire and develop others.

C. **Excuses leaders make for not delegating**

1. I think I can do it better.

2. They want the credit for the results.

3. They are a "hands-on" type of leader.

4. They don't want to look as if they're not doing anything.

5. They don't trust anyone.

D. **Watch for time wasters – time consumers.**

1. **Telephone**: set aside a block of time for phone calls (use caller ID and an answering machine).

2. **People**: ministering to people by appointments will enable you to minister to more people in less time.

3. If we do not manage our time, someone else will manage our time for us.

4. Avoid distractions from priorities as much as possible.

5. Lack of goals and objectives causes you to be unaware of how time is spent.

6. Failing to plan daily and weekly.

7. Avoid the open-door policy.

8. Have a time limit on visitors or visits.

Conclusion: Structuring our time increases our energy level and reduces our stress level. **Lou Holtz said, "Preparation reduces pressure, and lack of preparation increases pressure."**

We owe it to God, our families and ourselves to be organized and efficient. "There is an opportune time to do things, a right time for everything on earth" Ecclesiastes 3:1-8, The Message Bible .

Lee Iacocca

Lee Iacocca was a busy man running the Chrysler Corporation. Even so, he knew the value of taking time off. "I'm constantly amazed by the number of people who can't seem to control their own schedules. Over the years, I've had many executives come to me and say with pride: 'Boy, last year I worked so hard that I didn't take any vacation.' It's nothing to be proud of. I always feel like responding: 'You dummy. You mean to tell me that you can take responsibility for an $80 million project and you can't plan two weeks out of the year to go off with your family and have some fun?'"

- *Lee Iacocca, An Autobiography* by Lee Iacocca and William Novak, Bantam, 1988, quoted in Lifeline, Summer 1997.

DEFINING A BIBLICAL WORD USING A KJV BIBLE CONCORDANCE

Introduction: Every believer should know how to use a Bible concordance. Here are a few tips on how to define a biblical word using the concordance.

1. Choose a word from the text you want to define. For our study the word shall be "experiment" as used in 2 Corinthians 9:13 in the King James Version.

2. Use Strong's Exhaustive Concordance to find out the Strong's number, which will be used to look up the term in a Greek-English lexicon (dictionary). After acquiring a Strong's number, we will now use it to define the word. For our study we will use *Thayer's Greek-English Lexicon of the New Testament*.

3. Now we know what the word means. Let's look at other verses in the New Testament that use the same Greek word to get an idea of how God uses that word in His communication to us and what other terms are used in translating that same Greek term. This is where we really can get a good understanding of a term's meaning. We can use a word study concordance, like Tyndale's.

4. You should have come up with the following: Experiment (KJV): Strong's number 1382; *dokime* = approved, tried character exhibited in the contribution (*Thayer's Greek English Lexicon of the New Testament*; page 154).

   • Other translations: "proof" (NKJV); "proving" (ASV 1901). Tyndale's Word Study Concordance shows *dokime* in the following verses (page 160): Romans 5:4 (experience twice); 2 Corinthians 2:9 (proof); 2 Corinthians 8:2 (trial); 2 Corinthians 13:3 (proof); Philippians 2:22 (proof).

A SYSTEM FOR READING THE BIBLE ALL THE WAY THROUGH

Reading Plan

Introduction: A good reading plan is a must when approaching the Bible. It gives you structure and an organized, systematic way of reading the Bible.

Revelation 1:3 (NIV) **-** "Blessed is the one who reads aloud the words of this prophecy, and blessed are those who hear it and take to heart what is written in it, because the time is near."

Blessed are they that read.

Blessed are they that hear it.

A Bible reading system that works

- If you read 5 pages a day – through in 365 days – 1 time a year

- If you read 10 pages a day – through in 180 days – 2 times a year

- If you read 15 pages a day – through in 120 days – 3 times a year

- If you read 20 pages a day – through in 90 days – 4 times a year

- If you read 30 pages a day – through in 60 days – 6 times a year

- If you read 60 pages a day – through in 30 days – 12 times a year

ENEMIES OF THE WORD OF GOD

Introduction: The Word of God is the bread believers need to survive spiritually. Satan knows the Word of God empowers believers. He will use anything to hinder the Word from impacting your life.

2 Thessalonians 3:1-3 (AMP) – "Furthermore, brethren, do pray for us, that the Word of the Lord may speed on (spread rapidly and run its course) and be glorified (extolled) and triumph, even as [it has done] with you, and that we may be delivered from perverse (improper, unrighteous) and wicked (actively malicious) men, for not everybody has faith and is held by it. Yet the Lord is faithful, and He will strengthen [you] and set you on a firm foundation and guard you from the evil [one]."

I. **Enemies of the Word of God**

   A. Satan

      1. **Mark 4:15** (AMP) – "The ones along the path are those who have the Word sown [in their hearts], but when they hear, Satan comes at once and [by force] takes away the message which is sown in them."

   B. **Affliction** (Greek, *thlipsis*) = tribulation, affliction, trouble, anguish, persecution, burdened, to be afflicted, a pressing, pressing together, pressure, oppression, affliction, tribulation, distress, straits. (Greek, *kakopatheo*) = endure hardness, suffer trouble, endure affliction, be afflicted, to suffer (endure) evils (hardships, troubles), to be afflicted.

      1. **James 5:13** (KJV) – "Is any among you afflicted? let him pray. Is any merry? let him sing psalms."

        • **The "afflicted" pray.**

        • **The "merry" sing psalms.**

   C. Persecution (Greek , *diogmos*) -persecution.

      1. **Mark 4:17** (AMP) – "And they have no real root in themselves, and so they endure for a little while; then when trouble or persecution arises **on account of the Word,** they immediately are offended (become displeased, indignant, resentful), and they stumble and fall away."

      2. **Mark 4:16-17** (KJV) – "And these are they likewise which are sown on stony ground, who, when they have heard the word, immediately receive it with gladness, and have *no root in themselves*, and so endure for a time (literally "season")." Because they have no depth of character and live shallow lives (that is, "no root in themselves"), they rejoice over God's Word for only a season before it is stolen from their hearts. Mark 4:17 - "When affliction or persecution ariseth for the word's sake, immediately they are offended." The word *offended* is the Greek verb, number 4624, *skandalizo* and means to put a stumbling-block or impediment in the way. This Greek word

is translated "to offend" thirty times in the New Testament. People who are easily offended and continually hold on to those feelings will allow their emotions to be affected and will never fully advance or walk in the things of God. Holding on to offenses will hinder their ability to receive the Word of God, which prevents them from growing spiritually and lessening their potential in the kingdom of God.

3. **Mark 4:18-19** (KJV) – "And these are they which are sown among thorns; such as hear the word, and the cares of this world, and the deceitfulness of riches, and the lusts of other things entering in choke the word, and it becometh unfruitful." **The Amplified** says, "The cares and anxieties of the world and distractions of the age, and the pleasure and delight and false glamour and deceitfulness of riches, and the craving and passionate desire for other things creep in and choke and suffocate the Word, and it becomes fruitless."

D. **The cares of this world:**

- Lust of the flesh

- Lust of the eyes

- Pride of life

E. **The lusts of other things entering in**

Mark 4:19 (AMP) – "Then the cares and anxieties of the world and distractions of the age, and the pleasure and delight and false glamour and deceitfulness of riches, and the craving and passionate desire for other things creep in and choke and suffocate the Word, and it becomes fruitless."

TOP TEN STUDY BIBLES

1. **The ESV Study Bible**: It is a Bible created by saints for saints, but any sincere student of the Word of God will find a life-changing transformation within every page.

2. **The NLT Study Bible**: For new converts or believers, the New Living Translation presents God's Word in everyday language that's clear and easy to understand.

3. **The Life Application Study Bible:** It is a study Bible to help you understand God's Word as you study and read. It teaches you how to apply God's Word to your everyday life, your occupation, family, friendships, circumstances and questions. It provides study notes at the bottom of each page.

4. **The Thompson Chain-Reference Bible:** It is a Bible with a reference system that follows any subject, person, place or idea, from the start of your Bible to the end.

5. **The Hebrew-Greek Key Word Study Bible**: This Bible will help you understand the extensive vocabulary and elaborate structure of the original Hebrew and Greek languages. It includes Strong's Concordance numbers, exegetical notes, lexical aids and much more.

6. **The Message Bible:** A Bible that brings the Word of God into everyday life and is relevant to your life in today's society.

7. **The Audio Bible Dramatized CD**: An audio Bible for those who have busy lives. You can listen to it on the way to work or while sitting at your desk in the office.

8. **The Amplified Bible:** A Bible that gives the meaning of Scripture in the original Greek and Hebrew language.

9. **The Starting Point Study Bible**: A Bible for new converts who recently rededicated their lives to Christ and need to make a new beginning in their lives.

10. **The Comparative Study Bible**: Compares four major translations—the New International Version, the New American Standard Bible, the Amplified Bible and the King James Version.

CPSIA information can be obtained at www.ICGtesting.com
Printed in the USA
LVOW091922190513

334418LV00002B/2/P